Out and About

The Railway Station

Sue Barraclough

Photographs by Chris Fairclough

FRANKLIN WATTS
LONDON • SYDNEY

First published in 2006 by
Franklin Watts
338 Euston Road,
London NW1 3BH

Franklin Watts Australia
Hachette Children's Books
Level 17/207 Kent Street
Sydney NSW 2000

ISBN-10: 0 7496 6915 2
ISBN-13: 978 0 7496 6915 7

A CIP catalogue record for this book is available from the British Library.
Dewey Decimal Classification: 385.3'14

Planning and production by Discovery Books Limited
Editors: Paul Humphrey, Sue Barraclough
Designer: Jemima Lumley
Photography: Chris Fairclough

The author, packager and publisher would like to thank Arriva Trains, Wales for their help and participation in this book.

Printed in Malaysia

Franklin Watts is a division of Hachette Children's Books.

Contents

 The railway station

A **railway** station is a place where trains pick up and drop off **passengers**. You can also buy tickets and get travel information.

Lots of different trains stop at this station. Fast trains travel long distances across the country from one city to another.

Slower trains travel shorter distances between local towns.

There are several **platforms** in the station. These are the places where the trains stop so passengers can get on and off.

52835

People sit and wait on the benches for their trains to arrive at the platforms.

The team

Jan is the station **manager**. He is on the right of this picture, talking to Stephen, the platform **supervisor**.

Jacquie is a cleaner. She makes sure all the different parts of the station are tidy and clean.

Some staff work in the busy ticket office.

Alan works as a train **dispatcher**. He works on the platform checking the trains and signalling when it is safe to leave.

Brian works in the travel centre, helping people to plan their journeys and selling tickets.

Transport police

The transport police provide a police service for the railways across the country. They work to keep the railways safe and free from **crime**. The transport police **patrol** railway stations to make sure people know they are there to help.

🚆 Starting the day

There are lots of different jobs to do at the start of the day. At the **depot**, close to the station, a train is filled with fuel ready for the day ahead.

Gail works on the trains selling food and drinks. She fills in her **timesheet** before she starts work.

At the station entrance, a **security guard** empties all the money out of the ticket machine.

In the travel centre, Beth makes sure there are plenty of **timetables** for people to pick up.

The station manager

As station manager, Jan starts his day working in his office. His job is to make sure the station runs smoothly. He often goes to meetings to talk about changes and improvements to the train service.

🚆 At the main entrance

This is the station ticket office. People **queue** to buy tickets for their journeys.

This station also has ticket machines, which people can use to buy tickets.

The staff in the travel centre help people to choose the right tickets. Beth (left) checks the train times on her computer, then she prints out the tickets.

There are big timetables so passengers can find out train times when they arrive at the station.

Travel information

At the station people can pick up leaflets and timetables to give them all the information they need about travelling on trains.

Catching a train

This station has **barriers** so no one can get on to the platform without a ticket. You put your ticket in a machine to open the barriers.

Darren works at the barriers. He checks tickets and helps passengers to find the right platform for their trains.

This family are checking their tickets before they set off.

Tickets give information about your journey. If seats have been booked, the ticket shows the **carriage** and seat you will be sitting in.

Everyone waits on the platform for their train to arrive. Passengers stand well back from the edge of the platform as the train pulls in.

Getting information

The station information centre has **closed-circuit TV (CCTV)**. This helps Stephen to find out what is happening on all the platforms.

Sometimes there are last-minute platform changes. Stephen uses a **tannoy** to make an announcement to the passengers on the platforms.

Stephen also works on the help desk. The man on the left is partially-sighted so he cannot read the signs around the station. Stephen takes him to the right platform to catch his train.

Station signs

In a busy place like a railway station, signs are important. They help people to find their way around.

Alan, the train dispatcher, watches the passengers get on and off the train. He also helps passengers find their way around the station.

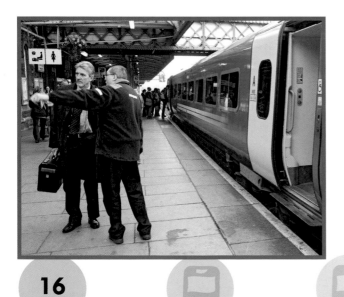

When it is time for the train to leave, the train doors close. Alan blows his whistle to let people know the train is ready.

Then Alan holds up the white side of his bat to show the driver all is well and that the train can leave the station.

Driving a train

David is a train driver. He arrives at the depot to collect his train. He has to carry out some checks on the train before he can drive it.

Once all the checks are done, David climbs into the train.

'We work with the platform staff to make sure the trains arrive and leave on time, and that the passengers get on and off safely.'
David, train driver

In the driver's cab, there is a big panel of controls that David uses to drive the train.

As the train arrives at the station, David slows the train down so it stops beside the platform.

The doors are opened so the passengers can get off and on.

David waits for the signal from the train dispatcher before he drives on.

David moves the train slowly away from the platform and then speeds up as the train gets further away from the station.

 Food and drinks

This station has a café that sells
food and drinks to passengers.

Before a train arrives
there is often a
queue of people
waiting to order
something.

Nancy works in the café making
hot drinks and snacks.

The **catering** team take trolleys on to the trains, so that people can buy drinks and snacks as they travel. Gail checks her trolley before she sets off to catch her train.

Gail uses the station lift to get the trolley to the right platform.

'The trolley is very heavy so I make sure I have plenty of time to get to the right platform.'
Gail, catering staff

Then Gail waits on the platform for her train to arrive. Once the train has stopped, she uses a **ramp** to get her trolley on to the train.

Patrolling the platforms

Steve is a transport police officer. He has been called to the station. A radio message says a bag has been left on the platform.

Alan tells Steve where the bag has been found.

Steve does not touch the bag, he radios through to the **control centre** for help. Just then, the owner hurries over to claim his bag.

'If you see a bag left on the platform, report it to station staff. Do not touch it.'
Steve, transport police officer

When Steve is out on patrol he helps passengers by giving them directions.

The transport police office

The transport police have an office at the station. Police officer Monty is checking some information on football fans who may travel through this station. The police make sure there are officers at stations crowded with fans.

Busy train tracks

Passenger trains come and go along the **tracks** all day.

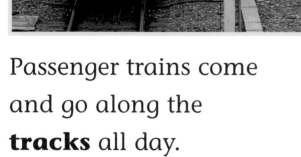

There are also slower trains that carry **freight**. These trains often run at night, when the railway tracks are clearer.

Train safety

Always stand back from the platform edge until your train has stopped.

In some stations, there is a line to show how far back from the platform edge to stand to be safe.

Remember to mind the gap between the train and the platform when you are getting on and off trains.

'Trains are fast and very heavy, so they cannot stop quickly. Children have been killed taking shortcuts across the tracks to school.'
David, train driver

On some railways there is an extra, electric, rail. For this reason, and because of all the train traffic, it is never safe to cross the tracks.

Passengers must not pass this point or cross the line

Danger
Do not touch the live rail

 # At the depot

At the depot, there is a huge shed where the trains are checked and **serviced**.

The trains are driven into the shed. They are parked over a pit that runs under the train. This means that the **mechanics** can work on every part of the train easily.

Trains are **refitted** at the depot. When an old train is refitted, parts such as seats and flooring are taken out and new parts are put in.

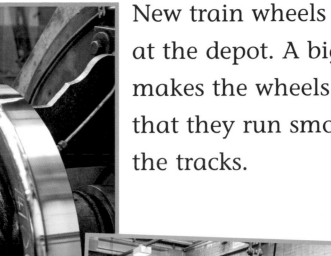

New train wheels are made at the depot. A big machine makes the wheels round so that they run smoothly along the tracks.

The train wheels are so heavy that they have to be lifted out of the machine with a big **hoist**.

Then the wheels are lined up, ready to be fitted onto a train.

At the end of the day

At the end of the day, Jan writes up some notes for a meeting the next day.

Trains are driven through the train wash, before they are parked at the depot.

Jacquie and Alan sweep and clean the platform.

Monty and Geoff write their reports in the transport police office.

David climbs down from the driver's cab at the depot.

Stephen changes out of his uniform, and he is ready to go home.

 # Glossary

barriers gates to control people getting into somewhere.

carriage the part of the train where passengers sit.

catering making and serving food.

closed-circuit TV (CCTV) a camera that records what happens in certain places.

control centre a place where 999 calls are answered. The operators pass the calls on to the best police team to deal with the emergency.

crime doing something that is against the law.

depot a place where machinery is stored.

dispatcher someone who sends something away.

freight heavy goods.

hoist a device used to lift things.

manager someone who is in charge of a place of work.

mechanics people who mend machines.

passengers people who travel in cars, boats, trains or planes.

patrol to go out to check that all is well in a certain area.

platforms raised areas at a railway station where passengers get on and off trains.

queue to wait in a line.

railway a transport system, the trains run on steel rails.

ramp a flat piece of metal or wood used to wheel things up and down.

refitted remake something as good as new.

security guard a person who collects and delivers large amounts of money.

serviced work on something to make sure it runs well.

supervisor someone who is in charge of a team of workers.

tannoy an apparatus that makes a voice sound louder, used to send messages.

timesheet a piece of paper to write down the time worked.

timetables lists of times when trains arrive and leave.

tracks the steel rails that trains run along from station to station.

Further information

Websites

www.arrivatrainswales.co.uk The station in this book is run by Arriva Trains Wales. Visit this website to find out more.

www.nrn.org.uk Find out what's on at the National Railway Museum, and play some train games.

www.trackoff.org Facts and figures on train crime and safety, and a useful photofile.

Books

Trains (Need for Speed series), Chris Maynard, Franklin Watts, 2003

Train Journey (Follow the Map series), Deborah Chancellor, Franklin Watts, 2005

Every effort has been made by the Packagers and Publishers to ensure that these websites contain no inappropriate or offensive material. However, because of the nature of the Internet, it is impossible to guarantee that the contents of these sites will not be altered. We strongly advise that Internet access is supervised by a responsible adult.

Index